THE MECHANICS OF HANGING

By

JAMES BARR, M. D.

A MODE OF EXECUTION

ISBN-13:
978-1727076264

ISBN-10:
1727076265

THE MECHANICS OF HANGING

As the subject of the mode of carrying out executions has recently engaged public attention, the present is perhaps an opportune time for discussing the question in its scientific and humane bearings, so that some more definite ideas may prevail as to the best method of hanging, and that the details may not be entirely left to the caprice of the executioner. When the law requires the death-sentence to be meted out at the end of a hempen rope, the dictates of humanity demand that all the details should be carried out in "decency and in order," and with a minimum amount of suffering to the culprit, and from this stand-point I shall treat the subject.

The mode of carrying out the sentence of the law, "be hanged by the neck until you are dead," has usually been left to the discretion of the hangman, the law taking no cognizance as to what is to be the proximate cause of death. Calcraft invariably adopted the short drop of about two feet and a half; and if I may judge from some specimens of his ropes, which are still to be seen at Kirkdale, death must have been produced by a slow process of asphyxia. Marwood adopted what is generally known as the long drop, of which he was supposed by many to be the originator, though it was used long before his time, both in Paris and in Ireland.

To Professor Haughton we are indebted for a scientific exposition[1] of the *rationale* of the long drop, and of the mode in which death takes place. Dr. Haughton also gives an elaborate explanation of the American method, which is a scientific modification of the old naval method of running the culprit up to the yard-arm.

Having now briefly referred to the different modes of hanging which have been adopted in executing criminals, we will be better able to judge which is the best and most practical method when we have considered the various causes of death. Professor Tidy[2] says that "in hanging, as in drowning, death does not always take place in exactly the same way. Thus, it may result from (1) asphyxia; (2) cerebral hyperæmia; (3) a combination of asphyxia with apoplexy; (4) syncope; (5) injury to the spinal cord and pneumogastrics (neuro-paralytic death)."

Professor Hoffmann,[3] of Vienna, says that, "in hanging, the noose does not press directly on the larynx and the trachea, but almost always slips between the larynx and the chin. In these cases the basis of the tongue is pushed upward, and pressed against the posterior wall of the pharynx, completely closing it. The most important agent, however, in this kind of death is the compression of the larger vessels and the cervical portion of the vagus nerve, the upper portion of the carotid being pressed against the transverse processes of the cervical vertebræ before it branches off into the external and internal carotids, and the inner coat of the vessel being ruptured. The jugular veins are compressed at the same time, and the brain can neither receive any more blood nor allow that which it contains already to flow away; its irritability is therefore extinct. The very important part which both the vagus and the vessels take in causing death by hanging is clearly shown through the following observations: 1. Loss of consciousness following immediately the compression caused by the rope at the moment when the noose is drawn tight by the weight of the body. The truth of this assertion is proved by the fact that no person who commits suicide by hanging ever attempts to rid himself of the rope which throttles him, although he might do so easily by standing upright, as the body is not always suspended above the surface of the ground. 2. The rapidity with which death ensues and the beating of the heart stops. The few struggling respirations which generally occur in asphyxia shortly before death have not been observed in persons who have been hung. It is also well known how difficult it is to restore such patients to life. Death by hanging is, then, complex. It results from the occlusion of the respiratory tubes, from the sudden interruption of the passage of blood into the brain, and possibly from arrest of the circulation determined by the compression of the vagi nerves." These observations of Professor Hoffmann obviously refer to cases of constriction of the neck without dislocation of the vertebræ, and show how death should take place rather than how it does in cases of the short drop. The constriction of the neck is not usually so complete as he has assumed; the carotids are not completely obliterated, as shown by the pulse in the temporal artery, and by the gradual increasing congestion of the head— owing to the obstruction to the venous return—until at last the tongue is protruded out of the mouth; nor is the vagus much pressed upon, as evidenced by the long continuance of the heart's beats in many cases. It shows rather a paucity of reasoning to infer immediate loss of consciousness because no suicide "ever attempts to rid himself of the rope which throttles him." A suicide is a very unlikely individual to change his purpose during the short period which elapses between suspension and loss of consciousness.

Dr. Taylor[4] states that "death from hanging appears to take place very rapidly, and without causing any suffering to the person. Professor Tidy, also, speaks of the painless nature of death from hanging; while Professor Haughton, in his paper read before the Surgical Society of Dublin, says that "the old system of taking a convict's life by suffocation is inhumanly painful, unnecessarily prolonged, and revolting to those whose duty it is to be present." Those who speak of the painless nature of death by strangulation arrive at this conclusion from the fact that many cases of suicide are not completely suspended, and that if they wished they could easily relieve the constriction by assuming the erect posture, and in other cases of recovery from attempted suicide by hanging there is no recollection of any suffering. It should be remembered, however, that there is a great difference between the mental attitude of the suicide and one who is about to suffer the extreme penalty of the law. In the former case he is regardless, and perhaps also not very sensitive, of a little suffering, while in the latter every nerve is braced up to resist the inevitable result. Moreover, in those cases of recovery the loss of recollection of suffering does not prove that there was none. It might almost as well be said that, because in many cases of recovery from meningitis there was no remembrance of any suffering, therefore there was none. No doubt, the pain in hanging can under no circumstances be very acute, yet when we see a culprit heaving his chest and almost raising the whole body in his struggles for breath we must conclude that there is at least a considerable amount of mental torture.

While death from asphyxia as ordinarily brought about by the short drop is a barbarism which should not be tolerated in this humanitarian age, yet it might be accomplished without much suffering. If this mode of death be determined upon, then the constriction should be complete, and the compression of the blood-vessels, both veins and arteries, and if possible also the nerves, is of even more importance in the production of rapid unconsciousness than the occlusion of the windpipe. In accomplishing this object the position of the noose is of importance; it should never be placed over the larynx, as the rigidity of that organ prevents complete compression and also shields the blood-vessels. Below the larynx would perhaps be the best position, but then there would always be the danger of the noose shifting up to the least desirable spot, therefore the most suitable position would seem to be between the hyoid bone and lower jaw. The rope should be thin and pliable, and not very elastic (a silk rope would perhaps be the best), the ring should be placed under the lower jaw, and the drop should be long enough to compress windpipe, blood-vessels, and nerves. If a half-inch silk rope were used I should think a drop of from four to six feet, according to the weight of the prisoner, would be sufficient. As to deaths from cerebral hyperemia, and its combination with asphyxia, they are merely modifications of the latter form of death, and result from incomplete constriction, the windpipe not being quite occluded, while the venous return is obstructed, but not the arterial supply. They are thus rather slow forms of death, and consequently not desirable. Death from syncope may be associated with any mode of hanging, but is perhaps most frequently connected with the long drop. It is about the most rapid and least painful, though perhaps the rarest form of death. In a case of syncope, I have seen the heart's action cease in two minutes from the time the bolt was drawn. Fear largely contributes to this mode of death.

It now remains for us to consider death by dislocation or fracture of the cervical vertebræ, with consequent laceration of the spinal cord. It is frequently supposed that the injury arises from rupture of the transverse ligament of the atlas and pressure on the cord by the odontoid process, but, if ever this does occur, it must be extremely rare. Rupture of the transverse ligament could only take place when the rope was adjusted very high in the neck, with the ring directly in front or behind. And even then the odontoid process would be more likely to break than the ligament. The destructive effect occurs at the point on which the strain is brought to bear, and so the seat of injury varies in different cases. I have seen it take place in the following situations: Complete separation between the second and third cervical vertebræ and fracture of the odontoid process at its junction with the body of the axis; oblique fracture through the body of the axis, leaving the upper fragment with attached odontoid process *in situ*, and fracture of the arch separating it from the body of the axis; complete separation between the second and third cervical vertebræ above the intervertebral disk, also slight separation and tearing of ligaments between the atlas and the axis; and complete dislocation between the fifth and sixth cervical vertebræ. In this latter case the ring hitched on the chin, and the opposite part of the noose was low in the neck, so that the long leverage action determined the low position of the injury. In every case the vertebræ were separated at the point of injury for at least an inch, the spinal cord was severed, and the vertebral arteries and all the ligaments were torn across.

The shock to the nervous system produces an immediate loss of consciousness, with complete paralysis of all the voluntary muscles. It takes a body moving under the influence of gravity three quarters of a second to fall through the space of nine feet; and, owing to the velocity acquired, according to the law of uniformly accelerated motion, the time occupied in the last seven inches—during which the stretching and tightening of the rope occurs—is only ·0225 of a second. If to this we add, say, ·0275 for the elasticity of the rope, then the whole time during which the shock could be felt is only ·05, or one twentieth of a second. Even from this we must deduct the time which it takes for the nervous impression to travel to the sensorium and back, but, as the nerve-current travels at the rate of one hundred feet per second, this is so slight that, like the atmospheric resistance to the falling body, it may be left out of account. Although loss of consciousness, and it is with this that humanitarians are chiefly concerned, is instantaneous, yet death, as evidenced by the cessation of the heart's action, does not take place so rapidly. It is possible in some cases that the cardio-inhibitory center may be stimulated, or the vagi compressed, so as to immediately arrest the beat of the heart, yet I am convinced that this is the exception, and not the rule. The respiratory and vaso-motor centers are at once paralyzed. I have never seen even the faintest involuntary gasp, and the arteries feel at once to have lost tone. The excito-motor ganglia of the heart keep up its action, in the majority of cases, for some minutes independently of the central nervous system, and its arrest is probably brought about by a process of asphyxia. The immediate cessation of all respiratory movements deprives the heart of all assistance in carrying on the circulation, and prevents the lungs from becoming surcharged with blood, as in ordinary cases of asphyxia, but the other signs of death from that cause are usually present, such as turgescence of the right side of the heart and general venous system; great lividity of the face; swelling, and perhaps protrusion, of the tongue. It should be remembered that these latter signs are best observed during suspension, because when the body is taken down hypostasis occurs quickly owing to the great fluidity of the blood, the tongue recedes within the mouth, and the general lividity on the upper surface of the body disappears, to reappear in the most dependent parts. The right side of the heart soon becomes incapable of driving the unoxidized blood through the lungs; the left ventricle at first readily propels the blood into the lax arteries, but soon the supply is diminished and the contraction becomes feeble, and at the same time the blood is accumulating in the venous system, and thus tending to equalize the pressure, and so at last the left ventricle is unable to drive its modicum of blood through the systemic capillaries. We have thus at the same time both sides of the heart unable to perform their work, and cessation of the cardiac action is the result. The time during which I have observed the heart's action after dislocation of the cervical vertebræ has ranged from two to thirteen minutes. As Professor Haughton has shown, the destructive effect on the neck of the criminal is in proportion to the *vis viva* which is acquired by the weight of the culprit and length of the drop; and, if the drop be long enough, the vertebræ are certain to be dislocated, no matter what be the position of the ring or thickness of the rope. The *vis viva* in any case is equivalent to half the mass multiplied by the square of the terminal velocity. Let W represent the weight of the criminal, and S the length of the drop, then the formula will be:

,

or the weight of the criminal multiplied by the length of the drop expresses in foot-pounds the amount of work expended on the neck of the criminal. I have not complicated the formula with the co-efficient of the elasticity of the rope—which is very slight—as we will devote some attention to the character of the rope further on. I would now modify Dr. Haughton's rules by substituting, say, 1,260 foot-pounds for 2,240. If the neck of the criminal be small and delicate, or the rope very fine, then it would be well to calculate on a lower basis—say, 1,120 foot-pounds. Thus, a man weighing 140 pounds would require a drop

of nine feet (   ), and one weighing 120

pounds should have ten feet and a half (   ). The rope should not be too thick nor too elastic, otherwise the abrupt shock will be broken, and the advantages of the long drop lost; but, on the other hand, it should not be too thin nor too inelastic, as then there is not merely the risk of the rope breaking, but also of snapping the head off the culprit. The rope should be of the finest and best hemp, pliable, and capable of bearing a strain of at least a ton and a half. About three fourths to seven eighths of an inch in diameter will be found a convenient thickness, and every rope should be tested before being used. I have been told by the master of a ship that, if in the manufacture of the rope the hemp be run through oil, it makes the rope much more pliable. It would certainly prevent it from becoming stiff when exposed during a wet morning. The iron hooks and couplings to which the rope is attached should be inspected on each occasion.

There has been a great difference of opinion regarding the position of the ring; Professor Haughton recommends that it be placed under the chin, while Dr. Barker, of Melbourne, would have it on the nape of the neck. When the ring is placed in the latter position, the chin naturally falls forward on the sternum, and the rope has no leverage action whatever to assist in dislocation; and, moreover, the noose does not tighten well on the neck, but the ring lies against the occiput; so this position is not only the worst for producing luxation, but also for strangulation. When the ring is under the jaw or chin there is a leverage of several inches, the head is thrown back or to one side, and the noose firmly constricts the neck. In the stretching of the rope the noose tightens several inches; if, therefore, the ring be placed under the angle of the lower jaw on either side, and directed forward, it will be drawn under the chin in the act of tightening. The noose should be placed as high in the neck as possible, and drawn just sufficiently tight to prevent it slipping out of position while the body is falling.

If those in authority would lay down a few simple rules as to the manner in which executions should be performed, then it would not require much *science* to carry them out. These rules might perhaps also have the effect of relegating the executioner more into obscurity, and dispel all illusionary ideas as to his being the possessor of a *mystic* craft, or one to be fêted by the populace and interviewed by the press in order to satisfy a morbid public taste.—*Lancet.*

1.

- "Principles of Animal Mechanics," 1873.
- • "Legal Medicine," part ii, p. 385.
- • "British Medical Journal," December 21, 1878, and May 10, 1879.
- "The Principles and Practice of Medical Jurisprudence," 1865, p. 651.